D1104277

YOU *CAN* JUDGE A BOOK BY ITS

COVER

SCOTT BLOOM

www.mascotbooks.com

You CAN Judge a Book by Its Cover

Exterior cover design by Matthew Gonsalves
Interior covers designed by Lissy Shapiro and Jimmy Lee Wirt
Author photos by Dustin Walker

For more information, please contact:
Mascot Books
620 Herndon Parkway, Suite 320
Herndon, VA 20170
info@mascotbooks.com

CPSIA Code: PRTWP0719A
ISBN-13: 978-1-64307-179-4

Printed in Malaysia

Special thanks to my real team of faux conspirators who shared their immense talents to help create this inspiring book of book covers: Brian Murphy, Lissy Shapiro, Jimmy Lee Wirt, Ben Carrizzo, Kiley Garrett, Matt Gonsalves, Sue Beranek, Chris Bonno, Andy Erdman, and Dawn Reif.

FAUXWORD

I remember the day Scott Bloom walked into my classroom at Manhattan College. He was taking my creative writing workshop, "The Writer's Journey." Ironically, our initial journey together didn't last long; he dropped the class after two weeks. However, in that brief period of time I saw in Scott the three essential characteristics that all great faux writers possess: first, ambition. Second, imagination. And third, basically a total disregard for reality. In the thirty-odd years since then, Scott has become a close friend, and our relationship as mentor and protégé has grown and led to some of the most thought-provoking book covers of the 21st century.

I feel fortunate to have witnessed Scott's ascent from fledgling writer to internationally-acclaimed faux author. When I first suggested he share his inspirational story, he rejected the idea. He thought that nobody would believe the autobiography of a faux writer. I persisted: "Tell your story and let the readers judge for themselves. Because I believe you CAN judge a book by its cover and no one epitomizes this more than, you, Scott Bloom." Why? Because with Scott, what you see is what you get. And what you're about to see in this curated collection of book covers will speak volumes about who Scott is as a faux author and how he got to where he is today.

Let me give you some background. Scott grew up in the suburbs of New York City and dreamed of one day becoming a famous author. In college, he wrote short stories, submitting his work to anyone who could read. He wrote for years without a published piece, literary agent, or any kind of recognition whatsoever. This haunted him and brought him to the brink of quitting on a daily basis. But he hung in there. I remember seeing him reading his own works and quietly laughing to himself somewhere between inspiration and insanity.

Anyhow, time passed since our first meeting, and Scott was still struggling to get notoriety for his own work. So, he branched out to try what he called "tribute authorship." He set about "covering" other authors' creations, penning such highly-unauthorized sequels as Stephen King's *The Green Mile After the First Green Mile, Only Greener,* and Tom Clancy's *Patriot Games and Other Fun Activities for the Whole Family.*

Sadly, he soon found himself entangled in legal battles with "well-known" authors who sued him for violation of intellectual property, copyright infringement, and what court documents called an "imbecilic misuse of page and ink." Literary critics dismissed his "tribute books" as derivative and unethical, but others often praised his powerful and provocative book covers.

Inspired by these fans, he reverse-engineered the writing process and focused on the book covers first. Scott conceived the title, then the book cover design, and followed it up with a blurb about the book. To ferment his imagination further, Scott would go to bed and let his subconscious write. The next morning, an entire manuscript would be etched in his brain. But rather than sitting down and typing it all out, he would let the entire completed manuscript drift back into humankind's collective unconscious. Only the covers interested him.

From that moment on, he never typed a single word in a single manuscript again. Thousands of years after the invention of literature, Scott had finally perfected a way of never needing to write a book again. He happily surrendered his dream of being a conventional "author," and found his niche as the Master of Faux. It is no exaggeration to say that my friend, Scott Bloom, is the single greatest faux author in the world today. And if you can't judge his books by their covers, then you can't judge any book by its cover.

– Brian Murphy, Professor Emeritus, Manhattan College,
Institute for Advanced Studies in Faux Literature

ORGANIZATIONAL LEADERSHIP

Life is about choices, and career development is no exception. You can claw your way rung by rung to the top of the corporate ladder. Or, you can choose to soar past rivals in your self-propelled Elevator of Greatness™.

This book examines the choices any ambitious professional must make on his or her dizzying climb through the jungle of leadership and organizational structure to reach the summit of Mount Org Chart. As the great American industrialist and inventor of the elevator Elisha Graves Otis said, "He who controls the elevator buttons, controls the whole car's destiny."

These pages reveal the ancient secrets of the Chinese Ascendancy Prophecy and the eternal principles of the survivalist doctrine, *Mind over Ladder*. Follow my 12 Floors to Ascendancy™ program and you will skyrocket to C.E.O. (Chief Elevator Operator) faster than you can say, "My floor!"

Next time you hear someone ask, "Going up?", realize it's a metaphysical mating call from the universe to your inner executive. It's beckoning you to hop into your personal Elevator of Greatness™, hit 'door closed', choose your floor, and then stand in front of the panel to keep would-be competitors from hijacking your express car to the top.

Ding! Your private elevator has arrived. Step in. Your destiny awaits...

REVISED EDITION

BONUS TECHNIQUES INCLUDED!

HOW TO CLIMB THE CORPORATE LADDER BY TAKING THE ELEVATOR

SCOTT BLOOM

WORKPLACE CULTURE

In this fascinating exposé on office politics, you'll discover how to negotiate the perilous terrain of workplace egos and micromanaging bosses.

Learn to make your voice heard over the demeaning, self-serving tirades of power-hungry superiors. Find your "I'm-mad-as-hell-and-I'm-not-going-to-take-it-anymore" confidence and take back control. Your actions today will impact your boss' opinions of you tomorrow. Stop being a victim and embrace the independent territorial philosophy of Cubicle Thinker's Mind™.

This handbook lays the groundwork for dismantling the manager-employee power dynamic, setting you free to pursue your most ambitious work-avoidance goals. Begin by organizing a members-only Cubicle Club, where bosses are not welcome and supervisors are turned away at the door (figuratively speaking since you don't have one).

The first rule of Cubicle Club: You do not talk about Cubicle Club. The second rule of Cubicle Club: You DO NOT talk about Cubicle Club. The third rule of Cubicle Club: If your boss comes by your desk and you're not there, everyone in the surrounding cubicles must engage in an actual *Fight Club* brawl as a distraction. This continues until you come back from your extended personal break, the boss walks away in disgust, or someone yells stop, goes limp, or taps out.

This book won several awards, including the Human Resources Book Prize and the Bill Lumbergh Literary Award for Exceptional Office Space Acumen.

I'M GETTING IT DONE! STOP COMING BY MY CUBICLE!

SCOTT BLOOM

SPIRITUAL TIME MANAGEMENT

"Time is an illusion."

– *Albert Einstein*

The Power of Later is a practical guide for those who want to experience timeless living. Sooner than you think, but later than you expect, your world will open up and your present life will align with your future expectations. Past mistakes will fade away and future opportunities will appear. Learn to recalibrate your internal clock to "later" time, so when you step into the future, you'll finally be present in the NOW.

Here's what critics and colleagues are saying about this classic bestseller:

"Eckhart Tolle and Marianne Williamson move over. There's a new spiritual self-help sheriff in town. And his name is Scott Bloom!"

– *Minneapolis Weekly Tribune Quarterly*

"Talk about a space-time reality check! A must-read for all past, present and future time travelers."

– *Metaphysical Times*

"I haven't yet read the book, but I will later… or sometime after that."

– *All of my friends*

THE POWER OF

LATER

A GUIDE TO SPIRITUAL PROCRASTINATION
Learn how to be Present in the Future

With a New Preface by the Author

OVER
2 MILLION
COPIES
SOLD

Scott Bloom

~

PERSONAL SUCCESS DEVELOPMENT

"Follow your bliss. Find where it is, and don't be afraid to follow it."

– Joseph Campbell, mythologist

After nearly two decades of pondering poets, scholars, and personal development experts, I felt obliged to borrow some of their concepts and design my own success model. While I was a bit stressed out about plagiarizing them, I did it anyway. Voilà! Bliss!

I realized that sitting around visualizing and breathing was a waste of time. If you need to be reminded to breathe, you shouldn't be accomplishing goals—you should be in an ICU.

High achievement is easily attainable by accepting stress. Forcing yourself to deal with contradictory desires unclogs pathways and leads you directly into the Garden of Actualization™—a safe place where possibilities grow and self-fulfillment blooms.

Although Joseph Campbell encourages us to find blissful existence, we're also here to get stuff done! In the workbook section, I teach you to analyze your Hierarchy of Positivity Pyramid Index™ (HPPI) and locate the stressful-nexus between selfish happiness and unselfish productivity.

Embody stress. Achieve life's accomplishments. Now! Hurry! The clock is ticking! Rewrite your personal myth as we take on this journey, accumulate our stress, and blissfully explode.

Stress
The New Bliss

How Happiness Gets in the Way of Getting Things Done

SCOTT BLOOM

SELF-IMPROVEMENT

"Practice makes perfect, but practice does not make a perfectionist."

– Albert M. Bloom, founder, The American Society of Absolute Perfectionism (and Scott's dad)

It took me almost (maybe, at least, more or less) 10 years, 5 days, 11 hours, 6 minutes, and 4 seconds to finish this book, but it's perfect! Everything about perfecting perfectionism is now within your grasp.

My father taught me that if it isn't perfect, it's wrong, but I didn't see that as pressure. His strict adherence to the religion of Perfectionism motivated me to work harder, stricter, and with an undying devotion to getting it right. Every day I ask myself, "What can I do to make my life even more perfect?"

Here's how you can do it: Simply and perfectly follow the explicit, tested, quality-controlled exercises to reprogram your brain waves and tune into perfection. It's all done through my proprietary process called Minding for Gold™, where you excavate raw nuggets of genius from your mind-mine and refine them into highly polished bars of perfection-bullion.

In a perfect world, everyone is perfect. But where is the perfection in that? Perfection is found within the imperfection that surrounds it. To quickly obtain perfect perfectionism, observe the flawed, unpolished, tattered, misinformed, underachieving people around you; watch what they do and then, without hesitation or distraction, do the opposite.

✓ Strive for perfectionism. Not everyone gets there, but for those who do, it feels like home.

~~PERFECTING~~

~~PERFECTING~~

~~perfecting~~

PERFECTING PERFECTIONISM

HOW TO GET IT RIGHT THE FIRST TIME

SCOTT BLOOM

SUCCESS MANAGEMENT

How badly do you want to win in life? If you hesitated for even a split second to answer, this book is not for you. As Arnold Palmer famously stated, "Winning isn't everything, but wanting it is!"

There are two kinds of people in this world: those who divide the world into two kinds of people and those who don't. These Life Dividers™ create success for themselves by dividing and conquering, while everybody else just sits on the sidelines and watches.

Egos Are for Winners is packed with interviews of the most successful people in business, sports, politics and entertainment. It delves into what makes them tick and answers the question: What makes a winner? Unanimously, every one of them, without a moment of hesitation, said in a word, "Me!" There wasn't so much as a suggestion that anyone else even contributed to their success. When these ego-dynamic individuals gaze in a mirror, they don't see their reflection; they see a winner reflected back in human form.

There's a reason that there's no "U" in narcissism and it's because it already has two "I's." After reading this book, you'll finally know what it feels like to be a winner.

"One of the best books I've ever written!" – S.M. Bloom

EGOS ARE FOR WINNERS

Putting Narcissism at the Top of Your To-Do List

(as you send everyone else to the bottom)

SCOTT BLOOM

PERSONAL EMPOWERMENT

"Fake it till you make it" is an effective and powerful mantra for those individuals who genuinely have the potential to succeed. However, if you're an "UN-person" (someone who is UN-motivated, UN-ambitious and UN-qualified), then you need to take a more pragmatic approach and just focus on the "faking it" part.

This personal empowerment book will boost your self-esteem by helping you accept who you really are (barely competent), as opposed to who society wants you to be (highly accomplished). After completing the first exercise, "How to live in a Cubic Zirconia Reality™", you will shift gears, move into the fast lane and begin to live an authentic representation of a successful life.

Many people diagnosed with clinical Impostorism doubt their accomplishments and have a persistent, often internalized fear of being exposed as a fraud. Fortunately (but equally unfortunate for you), you don't need to worry about that. This is not you. Those people have actually accomplished something significant. You, on the other hand, are still struggling to find your "thing" and live on your friend's couch. You are the perfect candidate to internalize this "faking it till you can fake it for real" technique.

Let your inner impostor lead the way so you can finally live your idealized life. Stop wasting time mastering your talents and start mastering the impression that you are talented. This is the real you. This is your Plan B.

Now, go out there and fake it for real. Your secret is safe with me.

from the author of the #1 New York Times Bestseller
MASTERFAKER: How to Make It Faster by Faking Mastery First

OWNING YOUR INNER IMPOSTER

LEARN TO FAKE IT BEFORE YOU HAVE TO

FAKE IT FOR REAL

SCOTT BLOOM

SUBLIMINAL MARKETING

Adweek, Brandweek, and *Advertising Age* all voted this book to be the #1 Marketing Publication of All Time. It was on the Amazon Top 25 Business Books for 152 consecutive weeks. *Rhetoric Weekly* says, "Every marketer must own a copy today!"

Now, don't let these extraordinary accolades influence your decision to BUY THIS BOOK TODAY. Let all those thoughts drift away. Clear your mind. Breathe normally. Your eyes are getting heavy. Read my words. Slowly. One after another. Keep reading. Deep reading. You're getting the message. It moves you. It's powerful. You see this book sitting on your nightstand. See it. Look how comfortable it is there. How proud you are. You feel everyone envying your AWESOME DECISION to BUY THIS BOOK. Now imagine a mirror. See yourself and say, "Nobody tells me what to do. I make my own book-buying decisions." Look around, see the closest person to you, look them in the eye, and say, "I'M BUYING THIS BOOK because I WANT TO. And you should too!" Now, lastly, OWN IT! This is all you. Enjoy the moment.

You're on the verge of making the BEST DECISION of your adult life. Take a long slow deep breath... inhale... exhale... Read my words carefully as I count backwards from 10 to 1. When you get to 1, you'll awake feeling like a million bucks and ready to START READING YOUR NEW BOOK. 10... 9... 8... 7... 6... 5... 4... 3... 2... 1...

Warning: Do not read this book while driving or operating heavy equipment.

Author of the #1 bestseller
This Book Would Look Good on Your Desk

How to Deliver Subliminal Messages BUY the Book!

SCOTT BLOOM

Illustrations buy Will Purchase

MOTIVATIONAL BUSINESS

What do Bilbo Baggins, Frodo Baggins, and Samwise Gamgee have in common?

THEY GET RESULTS!

Hobbits are destined to succeed. It's their constant pursuit of something bigger than themselves that propels them to great heights. High ideals emanating from a low center of gravity creates a powerful wave of intention that fuels their ambition. *The 7 Habits of Highly Effective Hobbits* unique training method improves your personal effectiveness and productivity by aligning you with your true Middle-self™.

These diminutive creatures have confidence beyond their tiny stature, because they know that "size doesn't matter." To them, size is just a misguided earthly concept. Hobbits believe that "small-mindedness" limits our ability to achieve big goals.

Observe how these principally-centered, three-foot-tall powerhouses find the sweet spot in any challenge and zero in on their objective. Hobbits don't strive for the top. In fact, they can barely see the top. Instead, they head straight for the middle. And in doing so, they effect change in their lives and the individuals around them.

Get ready to venture beyond preconceived limitations as you shatter your ego-self and reemerge as your true Middle-self™. Through this simple paradigm shift, you can inhabit the same universal and timeless principles of Effective Mediocrity™ used by this ancient mortal race.

Integrate Hobbit Habits™ into your daily life and watch how small problems disappear and big things start to happen.

OVER 15 MILLION SOLD

THE 7 HABITS OF HIGHLY EFFECTIVE HOBBITS

With a New Foreword and Afterword by Bilbo Baggins

Powerful Lessons From Middle-Earth

"I did not give him permission to use this title!"
J.R.R. Tolkien – bestselling author of Lord Of The Rings

Scott R. Bloom

NEW THOUGHT & VISUALIZATION

Excerpt from Manifesting Like a MOFO:

> *One day. Not today. Not tomorrow. But soon. It's just a matter of time. It's definitely a possibility. More of a probability than a possibility. The "when" is inevitable. The "how" is conceivable. The "what" is achievable. And, the "why" is unbelievable. It doesn't make sense, but I know it's going to happen.*

In my 2018 self-help visualization bestseller, *Manifesting Like a MOFO*, I show you how to create the life of your dreams. As I was rereading the first chapter, "Motivation Mojo" this past summer, my own inspiring words jumped off the page, grabbed me by the collar and slapped me in the face. Twice! Excessive? Absolutely, but I needed this wake-up call. Immediately, I knew what I had to do. In a flash, the idea for *You CAN Judge a Book by Its Cover* appeared in my mind's eye. The following year a published book—the one that you're holding right now—manifested into existence.

If we are the authors of our own autobiographies, what legacy do you want to share with the world? Visualize your dream life. Write it down. Your publisher (aka the Universe) will take it from there. In no time, your Book of Life will move from the fiction section (dreams) into the non-fiction section (reality). Your life is now based on a true story. Yours!

Remember, when the universe has been served, it will start serving YOU. It's time to start manifesting like a **M**aker **O**f **F**uture **O**pportunities! All you need to do is say "when."

Manifesting *like a* MOFO*

Putting the Universe on Notice

*Maker of Future Opportunities

SCOTT BLOOM

MEDITATION & MINDFULNESS

Duuuuude! Seriously, dude! Ya gotta chill, brah. The stress is killing you, bro. You need to meditate pronto, dude.

I'm telling you, man. Meditation will solve all your problems. And the best part is... you don't have to do anything. You just chill like a Buddha statue and breathe. I'm totally serious, brah. That's it. It doesn't require any talent or experience or instruction or whatnot. Actually, the less whatnot the better.

In this awesome book I reveal these totally cool, mystical, eye-opening "closed eye" techniques to quiet your mind and open your soul. I can't believe I'm talking about your soul, dude. It's crazy, right?! I don't even know you, bro, but I guarantee you're gonna totally dig this.

Through my exclusive Lebowski Guided Meditation™ method, you'll experience an awakening of your Divine Dudeness. Simply find a quiet place in your man sanctuary, sit criss cross applesauce, flip your cap back to downward dog, turn ESPN down to low, close your eyes, and witness the opening of your Dude Chakra as you drift into a deep, meditative chill.

Native American shamans believe that as the dude abides, the Dude awakens. It's all in you, bro. Just let it out. You got this, brah! It's all Namaste from here.

Namaste, Brah!
A Totally Chill Guide to Awakening the Dude in YOU
From the bestselling author of
Do you Gu-ru? Unleashing the Self-Help Guru in YOU!
Scott Bloom

PERSONAL TRANSFORMATION

If you don't have time to read (and who does?), but still want to unlock the secrets of happiness, success, and your own powerful inner powerfulness (and who doesn't?), then you'll love this energizing self-help audio book.

In this 10th anniversary edition of *Who Moved My Chi?* I explore the mysterious, long-forgotten, buried, hidden, secret symbolism of the 22nd letter of the Greek alphabet, X (pronounced Chi and rests right between W and Y in our own "modern take" on letters). Join me as we examine how to reclaim our own internal X-factor from deep within our own mental X-files to change the circumstances of our own X-games, and enhance our total well-being and become our own enlightened X-Men and X-Women (pronounced Chi-men and Chi-women).

Deepak Chopra told me personally (in a dream I had last night) that this was "one of the most life-changing books that he has ever listened to in his car."

10th Anniversary Edition - Now With New Material

An Energizing Way to Deal with Change in your Aura and Life Force

Who Moved My Chi?

SCOTT BLOOM, M.D.

Foreward by Jimmy Lee Wirt Ph.D.

Read by
Chi-Chi Rodriguez

Featuring A
10th Anniversary
Interview With
Scott Bloom's
Inner Child

INNER CHILD DEVELOPMENT

We often fail to nurture our inner child and reject its existence until our Inner Youngster™ feels neglected, disparaged, and abandoned.

Consider the last time you pinched your Inner Rascal's™ cheeks or "got its nose." Think about how the lack of dueling grandparents bent on outdoing each other as "Santa's helpers" made you feel less than spoiled. That emptiness coupled with the heartache of no longer hearing, "goochy goochy goo" felt like a splinter in the finger of your heart. And you longed for some sweet elderly relative to kiss your boo-boo and make the pain go bye-bye.

Time to become your Inner Kiddo's™ grandparent.

With my revolutionary approach, you'll discover the benefits of becoming your inner child's Inner Grandma™ or Inner Grandpa™. You'll be "going for ice cream," "picking out toys," and "riding the merry-go-round" with your precious Inner Monkey™ in no time.

You won't be some holiday, birthday, or phone-calling part-timer, you'll spend quality time with your Inner Buddy™. You'll re-learn things like fishing, making funny faces, or getting to steer the car while sitting on your own lap.

Next time your therapist brings up your "inner child," politely tell her that your Inner Munchkin™ already feels loved by someone who truly accepts him, and he'll be spending the rest of the session at his Inner Grandparent's™ condo.

Then walk out the door and never look back. Your work is done.

SCOTT BLOOM

SPOILING YOUR INNER CHILD

How to Be Your Own Grandparent

RECOVERY & ADDICTION

"Once you start reading *How to Make Breaking Addictions a Habit*, you won't be able to put it down."

–*Anonymous*

Everyone falls somewhere on the addiction spectrum. And you, my friend, are no exception. Bad habits are tempting us at every turn. There's no escape. Discover how to exploit your obsessive-compulsive behavior and use it to your advantage. Choose recovery as your newest jones and become a recovery addict.

Start by reading this book over and over (and over) again. Indeed, buy multiple copies. Parcel the information to friends by selling them incomplete chapters. Give them a taste and they'll be back for more. Charge for the "re-ups" and this becomes a money-making machine. Invest in more books, so your reading habits "literally" pay for themselves. Imagine consuming powerful, mind-blowing wisdom daily without any guilt whatsoever.

In no time you will have a successful cartel with hard working "book smart corner boys" distributing your product to literary junkies everywhere. And don't worry about getting addicted to this book. The easy-to-follow 13 step lesson plan (included) teaches you how to break any addiction that pops up. Remember this guiding principle from the first step: "When it comes to knowledge, it's all right to get high on your own supply."

Make reading this book your new habit. Get off the hamster wheel of self-destructive behavior and join the thousands of healthy individuals who now live freely within their own Habitrail of Recovery™.

How To Make Breaking Addictions A Habit

Scott Bloom

HEALTH & WELLNESS

Imagine a diet regimen comprised of only disco fries, cheese steaks, pork rolls, hot sausages, Italian hoagies, pizza, and fried dough pastries.

In my fourth self-help diet book I show you how you can eat whatever you want and still gain weight. And, here's the secret. SPOILER ALERT! Once you realize that your weight is not the problem—it's your thoughts—your life will change.

Will you have the courage to let (yourself) go?

THE SOUTH JERSEY BEACH DIET

Lose Low Self-Esteem First!

The High Carb, High Fat, High Sugar, Low Protein Diet

Scott Bloom

Author of the *The Fatkins Diet* and *Body Fat for Life*

MARKETING ANALYSIS

Hot off the griddle is my definitive business case study on the Hotcake and why they sell so quickly.

Call them hotcakes, pancakes, griddlecakes, or the ubiquitous flapjack, when smothered in sweet butter and dripping with syrup, you know they taste damn good. But what you don't know is how, since their inception in the 1st century, these multi-platinum-selling, starch-based batter-disks became an omnipresent cultural phenomenon. And what you want to know and harness is the power that's kept them flying off shelves for 2000 years.

You'll learn how hotcakes became the legal tender of choice for ancient Greeks and Romans. You'll understand how, during the Elizabethan era, the Hotcake flipped over and battered the economically steadfast scone to serve up the Golden-Brown Age of Enlightenment. This historical treatise hashes through a cornucopia of juicy evidence to make your mouth, and your mind, water.

Marketing analysis hasn't been this hot since Mrs. Butterworth changed the shape of her bottle. This provocative tale of hotcakes and sales metrics reads more like a steamy romance novel than some didactic Harvard Business Review cover story.

Join me to break the fast of philosophical and sociological questions and feast on the meteoric rise-and-shine of the Hotcake and the mythology behind its record-breaking sales.

This book is not only a recipe on how to grow a business from the stack up, it's a wake-up call for you to step up to the plate and Batter up!

THE HISTORY OF
HOTCAKES
AND WHY THEY
SELL SO QUICKLY

Scott Bloom

FROM THE AUTHOR OF THE #1 BESTSELLER
Hotcakes are Flying off the Shelves
Why Mixed Metaphors Don't Work

ULTRA-MODERN LITERATURE

Witness the birth of a groundbreaking literary style. I present to you the No Words™ series of ultra-modern literature. Experience a new kind of fiction where pages are empty, but minds are full. A book filled with untapped story potential and unlimited character development. No words to manipulate your thoughts or imprison your imagination in some writer's finite world of mediocre, unoriginal word selection.

As co-authors, we create the infinite storylines, we explore the infinite plot twists, and we generate the infinite denouements of our infinite array of infinitely definitive characters. We'll rejoice in each new discovery as our boundless imagination devours every wordless, virgin page. Follow me down countless rabbit holes filled with mind maps untethered to wordy limitation to produce profound works of intimate art that only we understand. Indeed, after this book, you'll never look at literature the same way.

I HAVE NO WORDS

When There's Nothing Left to Say

SECOND EDITION

Available in 12 Languages

"350 blank pages of inspired genius"
– Steven Spielberg

"Mysterious! Evocative! Hauntingly void!"
– Stephen King

Now Available in Braille
"Smooth..." – Stevie Wonder

SCOTT BLOOM

HORROR TRIBUTE

I have wanted to cover this classic for years. The horror genre has never been my forte, but I wanted to stretch my tribute writer legs a bit. In this reimagining of *The Shining*, I was able to capture the haunting essence of King's novel, while still maintaining my own personal style and integrity. I know I hit a nerve with some of his diehard fans, but as a serious tribute author, there's a need to take risks and grow as an artist. I'm extremely proud of this book, considering that I had never read the original and I haven't seen the movie version in over 35 years. Somehow it all came back to me like the flooding of a blood-filled elevator.

My literary agent gave Stephen King an advance copy this past summer. I didn't know if King would read it, but just last week I received a handwritten note from him. It simply said: "Scott, I have to be honest with you. I didn't think you could pull it off. But after I read the first few pages, I was hooked. I don't think I've ever read something so beautiful and yet horrifying in my entire life. Your version of my story brought tears to my eyes. Congratulations, my kindred spirit!"

Wow! I couldn't believe my eyes. A handwritten note of praise from the King of Horror himself. I was speechless. I had no words. At least none of my own.

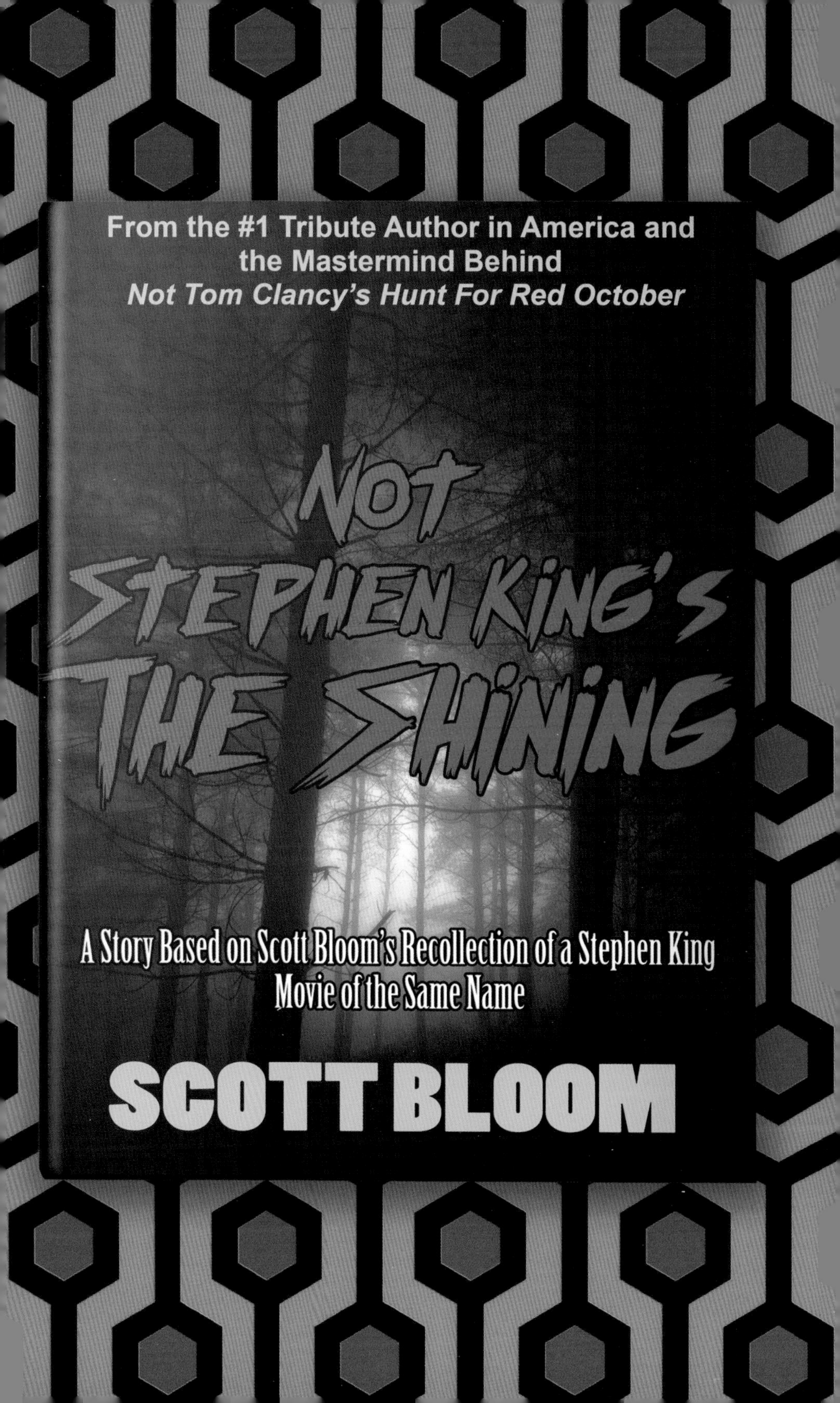
From the #1 Tribute Author in America and
the Mastermind Behind
Not Tom Clancy's Hunt For Red October
Not
Stephen King's
The Shining
A Story Based on Scott Bloom's Recollection of a Stephen King
Movie of the Same Name
SCOTT BLOOM

READING COMPREHENSION

Transform yourself from a "reading slacker" into a "literary junkie" in just 7 days.

If you crave knowledge and better comprehension but hate reading, you're not alone. Millions of people around the world suffer from RADD (Reading Attention Deficit Disorder). Luckily, there's an easier way. In my revolutionary new book on the Science of Reading, I show you how to read less and learn more in a fraction of the time.

Working with top linguistic scholars, I developed a state-of-the-art reading comprehension system called Photosynthetic Word Retention™. This scientifically-proven method enables you to SpeedScan™ 24,000 words per minute with 95% retention.

Here's how it works. They say a picture is worth a thousand words. That makes every image you see the equivalent of reading 1,000 words (or roughly four pages of an average book). The Photosynthetic Word Retention's™ audio guide retrains your brain to read in pictures.

This 7-Day introductory course will have you reading a 250-page book in less time than it takes to cook an egg. By using simple ocular exercises, you will sharpen your VKS skills (Visual Knowledge Screening) to the point where you will read 10–15 books an hour. Imagine reading faster than you can flip through the pages. It doesn't get any easier than this.

Welcome to the 21st century of picture-perfect reading! Finally, we're all on the same page.

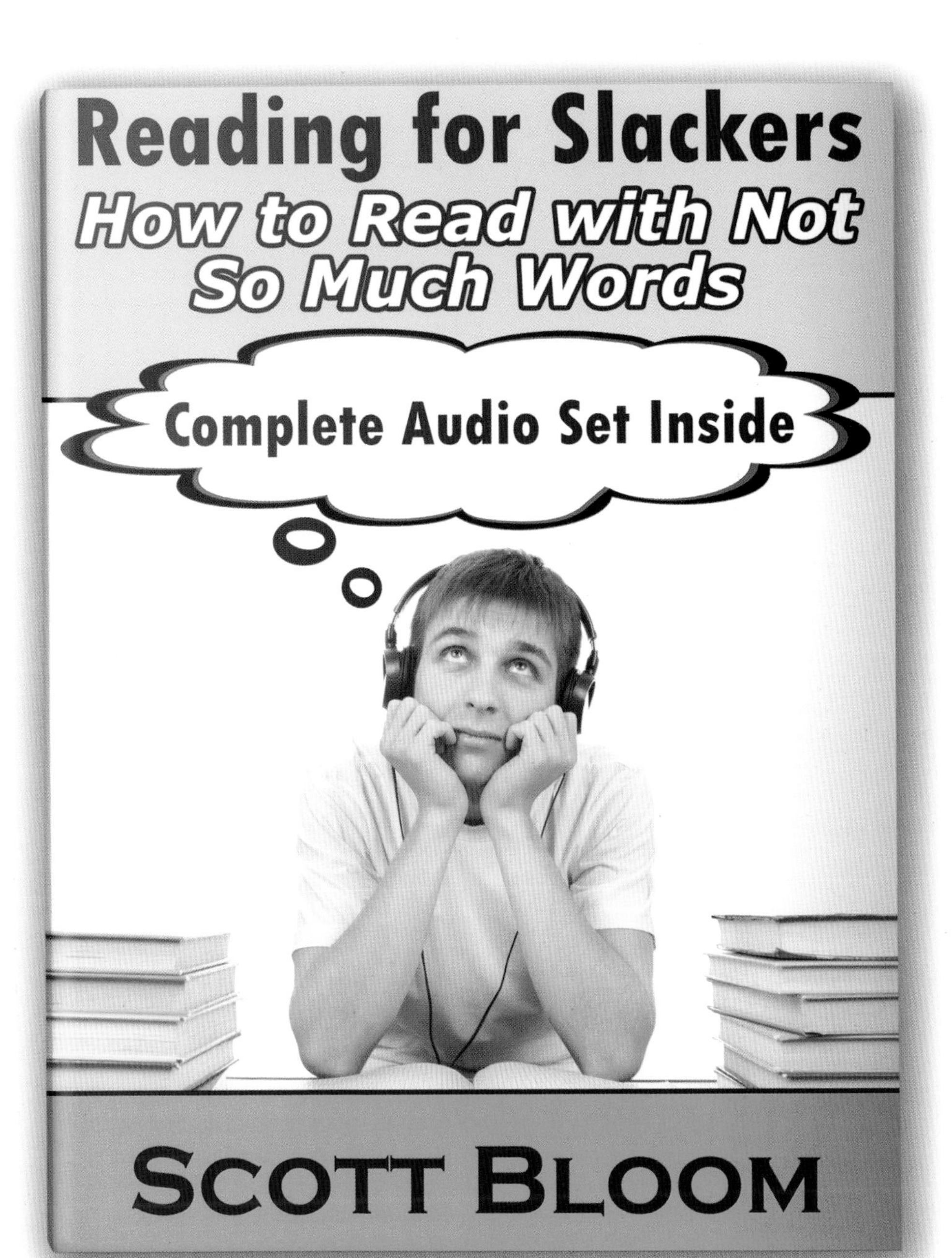
Reading for Slackers
How to Read with Not So Much Words
Complete Audio Set Inside
Scott Bloom

E-BOOK MARKETING

Did you know that 99.999% of all e-books in the world are sold online? What does that tell you?

It doesn't take a genius (or a Dummy) to realize that there is an incredible untapped market waiting to be discovered. This large type, picture-intensive reference guide will help you find your foothold in this uncharted mountain of opportunity. Cash in your Bitcoins today and start selling your e-books offline tomorrow.

Finally, a book written for dummies by Dummies.

The facts you need — fast

E-Books
FOR
DUMMIES®

How to Sell Your E-Book Offline

QUICK REFERENCE

SCOTT BLOOM

Author of ***Tax Loopholes for Dummies: How to Exploit the Gap Between Illegal and Unlegal***

Coming Soon:
Authentic Looking Book Covers for Dummies

SOCIAL MEDIA

As the rap group The Beastie Boys loudly proclaimed (and I'm paraphrasing), "You've gotta fight . . . for your right . . . to be swiped right!"

In this book that some Influencers are calling the Social Media Bible, discover how to flood your notification box with everything from ego-stroking comments about your profile pic ("You're gorgeous!") to self-validating "Likes" from people you don't even remember friending.

Author's Note:

Luckily, I am free of this compulsive self-involved behavior. But with that said...

If it's not too much trouble, please post a comment about the book on Instagram, Facebook, Twitter, LinkedIn... or even Tinder. #Joking #Inappropriate #SwipeRightJustInCase I've been told by my publishers that I need to build a stronger social media presence. #NotDesperate #DialBackTheNeediness #ProjectConfidence In fact, I already have tons of 5-star reviews on Amazon #GoingViral #OffTheCharts

Hold on. I'm going to check my feeds...BRB...#Hopeful #NeedAWinToday #Optimistic

Alrighty... no new followers. No new posts. No new shares. And to make things worse, I just received a critical review on Amazon. #ThanksALotDad #Perfectionism #WTF I'm fine. I can deal with it. #NotTrue #Insecure #KeepItTogether It's all good in the neighborhood. #StupidSaying #NeedToTurnThisAround The truth is that I don't need the validation #PerSe, but it would help book sales. #NoPressure #YouDecide #HelpABrotherOut

Please like, comment, share, follow or subscribe. Do whatever feels right to you. I'll be fine either way. #Maybe GTG. TTYL!

#Grateful #Humble #AwesomeFans #BlahBlahBlah #Hashtag #ImExhausted

GOING VIRAL

How to Boost Your Self-Esteem by Getting More Likes, Favs, Follows, Comments and Shares

SCOTT BLOOM

PSYCHOPHYSICAL PHENOMENON

Before you can fully appreciate the significance of this breakthrough discovery, you must first understand the difference between the myths of pseudoscience and the testable hypotheses of real science. Pseudoscience suggests that active people get more things done than non-active people. Science adeptly destroys this myth by saying,

"SHUT UP, STUPID PSEUDOSCIENCE! YOU DON'T KNOW WHAT YOU'RE TALKING ABOUT!"

The new science behind Active Inactivity™ proves that accomplished people spend more time doing less and getting more done. In my latest book on psychophysical phenomenon, I scientifically dissect the theories behind the psyche's struggle to balance the desire for great achievement (active) with the biological imperative to preserve energy (inactive).

Renowned German theoretical physicist, Werner Heisenberg asserts that Active Inactivity™ happens at a quantum level and cannot be detected until it is released. His well-documented Heisenberg Uncertainty Timetable states that it's impossible to simultaneously know what you're going to do and when you're going to do it. This Uncertainty Conundrum creates the potential energy that puts action into motion (I'm sorry, pseudoscience. Did I lose you? Do you need me to slow down?).

By isolating our intentions and focusing solely on the outcome, we can bypass the limbic system's survival mechanisms (fear & inertia) and get what we need done without overexerting ourselves. This scientifically proven method known as Active Inactivity™ enables you to slow down your life and maximize your potential for success.

IN YOUR FACE, PSEUDOSCIENCE! REAL SCIENCE RULES!

THE SCIENCE BEHIND ACTIVE INACTIVITY

How to Get Nothing Done Fast

SCOTT BLOOM

DIRECTIONAL DEVELOPMENT

What is the quickest way to get from Point A to Point B? It's simple. Start at Point B.

In this directional development book, I show you how to activate your internal GPS (Goals, Purpose, Synergy) and map out the best route for your personal success. No longer do you need to ask for directions from friends, mentors or experts. You've got this! Get behind the wheel and start revving your engines. Then shift your passion into DRIVE, step on the accelerator and race towards your destiny. Opportunity is up ahead. No detours. No doubts. No delays. Keep moving forward and don't look back as past fears and limiting beliefs fade away in your rearview mirror. Plus, the further you go, the farther you'll get. You're now on the road to success. Enjoy the ride!

WHEREVER YOU GO
THERE YOU ARE
(but where the hell have you been?)

HOW TO GET FURTHER BY GOING FARTHER

SCOTT BLOOM

BUSINESS PSYCHOLOGY

Are you willing to look outside your Waffle Zone™?

In my first business psychology book, I take an in-depth look at your Ego Quotient™ and explore how it gets in the way of improving your Achievement Construct™. This new psychological model combines an understanding of the science of Human Egonomics™ with the empirical laws of the Déjeuner Principle™ to help individuals and organizations attain effective and sustainable performance by finding their Aye-Game™.

From the Author of
Honest Break-Ups - It's not me. It's You.

Leggo My Ego

LOOKING OUTSIDE YOUR WAFFLE ZONE

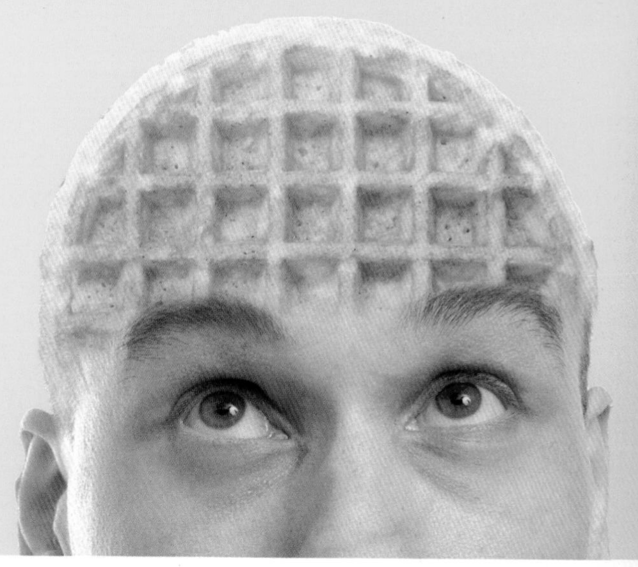

SCOTT BLOOM

INTERPERSONAL RELATIONS

Six weeks after this book's initial release, I sent an email to one of my closest friends.

Dear [redacted]

First, thank you so much for calling to congratulate me on the release of my book... oh, that wasn't you? I'm sorry. I must have gotten you confused with every other person in my life who took the time to congratulate me. My mistake.

In case you're curious, which I know is your strong suit... especially when it comes to other people... my newest book examines how self-involved individuals with passive-aggressive tendencies use backhanded compliments to express hostility in socially acceptable ways. Anyone in particular come to mind?

You know what I really admire about you? It's your honesty. You always say what's on your mind... even when nobody asks. I'm so psyched to hear your "constructive criticism" of my book. Your opinions mean so much to me, especially coming from one of the smartest people I know. I mean, who cares if you only have an online degree in Ergonomics from a community college? You earned it!

Enough about me. I hear you're so close to getting a publishing deal for your book. Gosh, I wish I had your patience. Remember, good things come to those who wait... and wait... and...

Btw, I loved your fedora the other week. Does it also come in adult sizes? I'd love to get one, too.

Warmest regards,

Scott

The Art of Being Passive Aggressive

HOW TO MAKE COMPLIMENTS HURT

SCOTT BLOOM

BUSINESS & MONEY

I recommend this business finance book to global CFO's, maverick entrepreneurs, small business owners, as well as first grade lemonade stand operators. Sometimes, all you need is common sense to grow your business.

Seven out of the top ten Fortune 100 companies have adopted this book as their Business Bible.

Stop working so hard and let your money work for you. Learn to relax and live your life on your terms. Don't let your life outlive you.

NATIONAL BESTSELLER

OVER 1 MILLION COPIES SOLD!

HOW TO INCREASE YOUR PROFITS BY MAKING MORE MONEY

SCOTT BLOOM

AUTHOR OF RICH DAD, ABSENT DAD

ENTREPRENEURSHIP & FINANCE

When does 2+2 NOT equal 4? Hold on to that thought for a moment...

Solving life's simplest mysteries often requires examining problems from a myriad of angles. Yet equating them to constant variables can sometimes spin out tangents that have tangents of their own. The next thing you know Galileo, Newton, Hawking, and Einstein are covering the blackboard of your mind with formulas and theories only they can understand (and they're dead). This is especially true when all you want is a bank loan.

In my latest book on trigonometric financing, I present an easy-to-read compendium of my calculations, musings, and discoveries on statistical models, wave equations, cyclical phenomena, and how these logically factor into the calculus of your ability to secure a line of credit.

You won't need to go *Good Will Hunting* once you become adept at the science behind the math. You don't need an abacus, a calculator, Excel, or even your own fingers because you'll know: 2+2 DOES equal 4!

Problem solved. The mathematical proof is in the pudding.

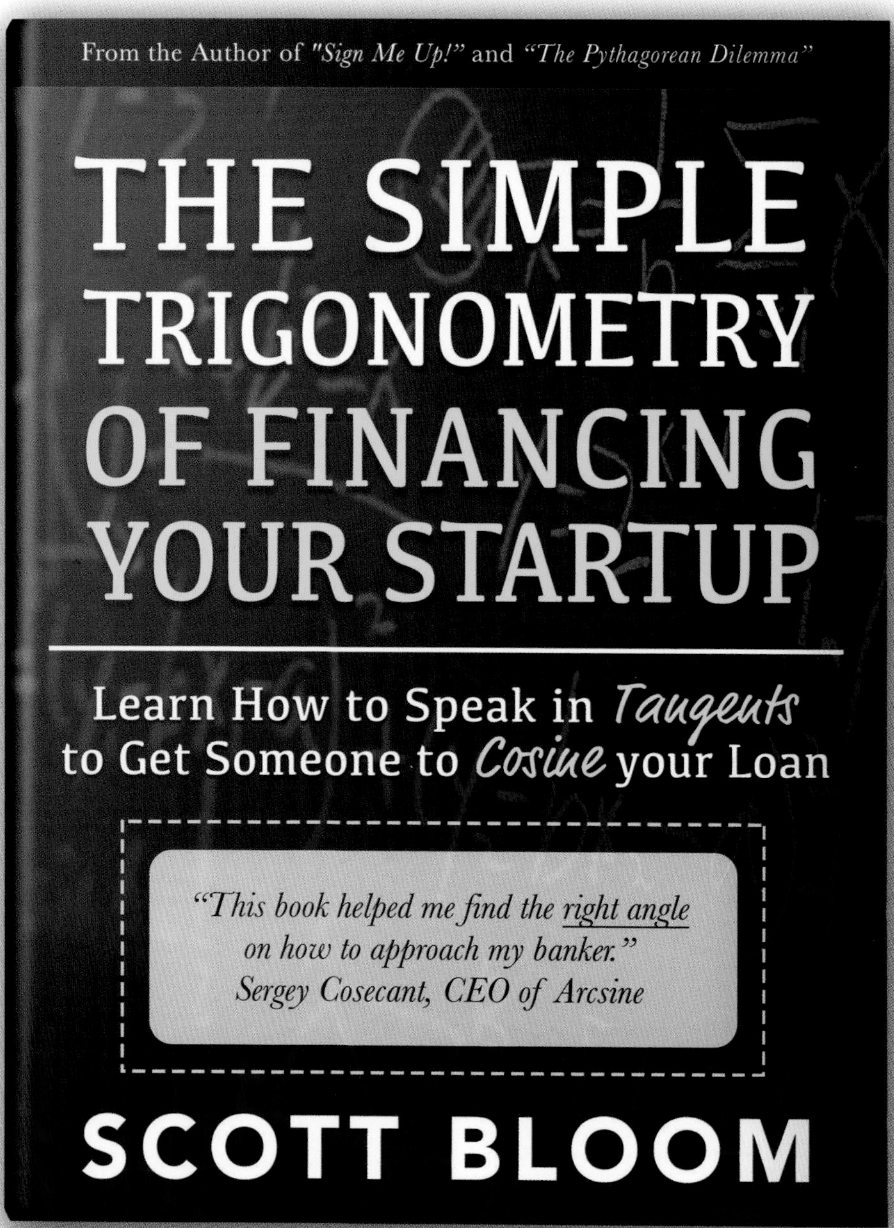

From the Author of *"Sign Me Up!"* and *"The Pythagorean Dilemma"*

THE SIMPLE TRIGONOMETRY OF FINANCING YOUR STARTUP

Learn How to Speak in *Tangents* to Get Someone to *Cosine* your Loan

"This book helped me find the right angle on how to approach my banker."
Sergey Cosecant, CEO of Arcsine

SCOTT BLOOM

LEADERSHIP DEVELOPMENT

"Maniac, brainiac, winning the game. I'm the lyrical Jesse James."

- Turbo B

When I close my eyes, I can still hear the lead singer of the '90s German Eurodance group Snap! belting out this refrain: "I've got the Power!" Four simple words, one flag planted, and millions saluting.

She meant business and in this ergonomically designed leadership development book (weighing in under the carpal tunnel threshold of 13.9 oz), I reveal my 9 Power Postures™ that embody a dynamic leadership style. Discover practical methods that project confidence, authority and effectiveness—without the risk of musculoskeletal injuries—as you sit comfortably yet assertively, behind a desk.

Learn to:

- ✔ Examine your Self-Destructive Weaknesses (SDW) and turn them into Form-fitting Strengths™ (FFS).
- ✔ Cultivate a leadership style that exudes a Strong Balanced Posture (SBP).
- ✔ Develop a Systematic Improvement Process (SIP) to boost your Leadership Confidence Index™ (LCI) even While Remaining Seated (WRS).
- ✔ Prepare Your Mindset (PYM) for the Massive Organizational Shift of Power (MOSOP) from mid-level management slouch to well-postured, confident, upright, and lower-lumbar supported player dominating the realm of executive leadership.

So, dust off your *Jock Jams* CD, slide it in your Walkman, turn up "The Power" and dance on over to your monster mahogany desk and plant your glutes in an ergonomically friendly Throne of Influence™.

It's yours! You've got the power! Now use it!

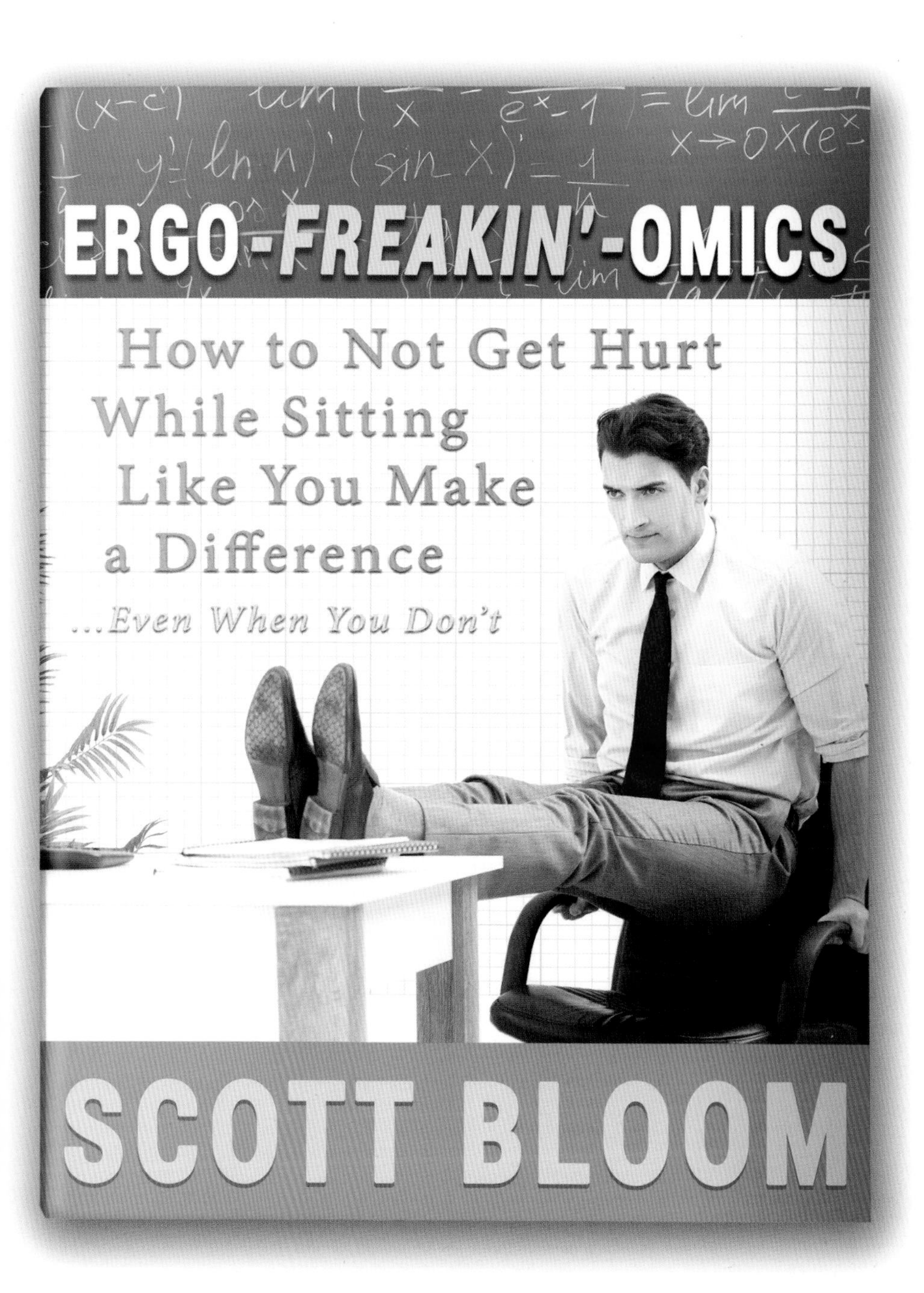
ERGO-FREAKIN'-OMICS
How to Not Get Hurt
While Sitting
Like You Make
a Difference
...Even When You Don't
SCOTT BLOOM

PROCRASTINATION FASCINATION

It took more time than expected, but I finally got around to writing my second book on the art of procrastination—which I wrote, primarily, as a way of avoiding other projects. Ah, there's an interesting idea, avoidance for the sake of... well, let me get back to that later.

Some people erroneously believe that procrastination is easy. Not true. Those Type A go-getters have never agonized for months thinking about starting project after project without pulling the trigger on a single one. It takes a dedicated, courageous individual to put their goals (and pride) aside and knowingly sit with feelings of self-loathing, despair, and guilt.

Next Stop, Procrastinationville takes the long, winding, roundabout journey to nowhere fast. It's a full speed ahead look back at time spent creating endless starts and stops, without getting anywhere.

Philosophers have long pondered this conundrum. After years in deep soulful procrastination, Confucius conceived this aphorism about man's internal struggle: "no matter where you go, there you are, so what's the point." One sec... I'll be right back.

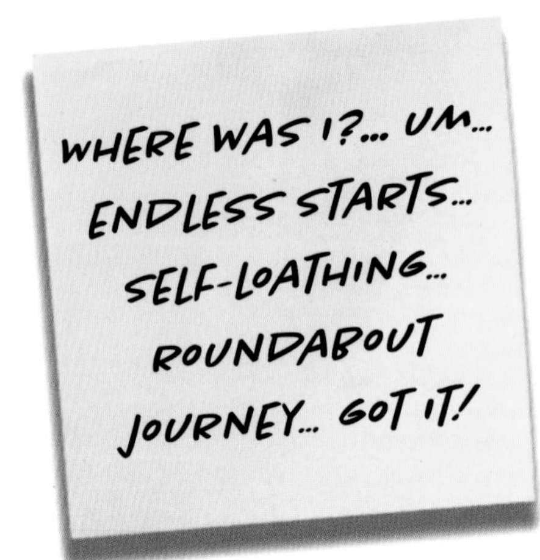

6 months later...

For professional procrastinators, it's not about the destination, it's about avoiding the journey. Sometimes Procrastinationville will be a stop along the way. Don't fight it. Unpack, settle in, unwind and let go. You're going to be here for a while.

Next Stop,

Procrastinationville

The Art of Waiting for the Right Moment, Then Letting It Pass

SCOTT BLOOM

CUSTOMER RELATIONS

"The customer is always right. ALWAYS?! Really? Think again!"

- Daniel Musk, disgruntled Tesla customer service rep and jealous younger brother of Elon

In this must-read book, I deliver a radical cutting-edge approach to customer service called Seller Centricity™. Sales professionals everywhere will benefit from proven customer disengagement techniques to create potent seller-centric relationships that enrich... YOU! After reading this book, you'll never look at customers in the same way again.

Publisher's Note:

Please be advised of our No Money-Back Guarantee policy. After purchasing this book, you own it for life. No returns. No refunds. No exceptions. Please don't call our customer service hotline. We won't pick up. Don't go to our website, VisionaryBookCovers.com*, and post a complaint. Nobody will respond. You should've read the fine print. Is that you calling now? There's no way I'm picking up... uh, Hello? Who's this? I already told you that you're not getting your money back. Uh-huh... yeah... well, good luck on trying to sue us. We publish down in the Caribbean for a reason. OK... whatever... uh-huh... I'm sorry this book cost you your business. How many customers did you lose? All of them? That's a first! When you commit, you really commit. Anyway, I wish I could help you out but it's not our policy. Good luck on your next business venture. And remember—the customer is almost never right... and this interaction just proved my point!*

THE CUSTOMER ISN'T ALWAYS RIGHT

BUT, OH, THEY SURE THINK THEY ARE

[The Magical Thinking of Consumers and the Problems Those Bozos Cause]

SCOTT BLOOM

BUSINESS STRATEGY

Small business owners make moves in a world where competitors aggressively target their clients to capture their accounts. When it's winner-take-all, they must step up their game and counter attack with positioning strategies that result in checkmate.

In my latest business strategy book, I show you ways to outsmart your competition by employing simple Cognitive Distortion™ tactics that destabilize your competitors while adding double-digit growth to your bottom line. Through a patented process called Reality Rendering™, you'll force rivals to question not only their reality but also their sanity, as they forfeit market share and bow their heads in defeat.

Imagine your competitors asking these unnerving questions: "Where did all my leads go? I swear they were right here a minute ago?!" Or, "Is this the correct address for my appointment? I was just here yesterday. Where did everyone go?!!" It's that easy.

Business is like a chess match. You need to be thinking 4 moves ahead (and know where to hide their queen when they're not looking).

Are you in it to win it? Then make your next move and purchase a copy* today!

*At this point, I cannot confirm or deny that there is an actual book to buy or if any of these techniques are actually legal.

Techniques for Gaslighting Your Competitors for Spite and Profit

Bonus:
The 10 best places to hide this book after you give it as a gift

Scott Bloom

DECISION MAKING & RISK BEHAVIOR

There are good decisions and bad decisions. Any do-gooder can make a good decision. Just take your time, ponder outcomes, consider options, and then make an educated, well-informed "choice." BORRRRRING! It takes courage, boldness, and impulsivity to overlook sound judgment and make a thrilling, life-altering bad decision. Discover how to experience the rapid release of dopamine without the side effects of shame, fear or regret. Cross over and become a Do-Badder™.

This extraordinary book shares scientific research on Risk Behavior Aptitude™, exploring and verifying the unadulterated joy in making the BEST bad decisions of your life. It's a step-by-step guide on preparing for that Moment of Compromise™, where you reject common sense and commit to an adrenaline pumping, heart racing, mind-melting, inexcusable decision—and do the unacceptably outrageous.

Together, we open the floodgates to reckless decision-making prowess, liberating your Inner Adventurer™ while simultaneously quelling those Dignity Demons™. Even though you'll experience only a 1.5 minute rush from these epic fails, you will enjoy a lifetime of vivid lurid memories to fall back on to re-stimulate your senses.

Make your first awesome bad decision by purchasing this book on my site, VisionaryBookCovers.com. Point. Click. Buy. I assure you that this one questionable decision will haunt you for the rest of your life.

What are you waiting for? It's time to start breaking bad today!

*If this is not the worst decision of your life, VisionaryBookCovers.com will refund you the entire purchase price (including shipping + handling). That's our Do-Badder Money Back Guarantee™!

From the #1 Author in the Country with Numbers in the Title

4 bad decisions *you can make* in under 10 minutes

SCOTT BLOOM

PSYCHOLOGICAL THRILLER

In this autobiographical self-help thriller, I venture beyond the outer limits of my comfort zone in search of the truth behind the origins of Me. Through extensive analysis of my narcissistic needs and desires, I uncover the remains of my authentic self, buried deep within the rubble of a shattered image of self-importance.

Join me on this personal journey to regain my self-esteem. Watch how I reestablish a connection with my abandoned Self and finally muster the courage to put my inner child in an extended, yet compassionate time-out. Along the way I encounter various mentor archetypes who share their enlightened wisdom with me. These awakened beings show me that self-realization without self-sacrifice leads to a lack of self-awareness and a rejection of self-transcendence. I quickly realize that without profound self-reflection I would drown in the glorification of my self-centered Self.

Hidden within the parables of this psychological whodunnit are the tools you'll need to face the dark side of your Shadow Self and reclaim the power of your true essence. People like to say, "There is no 'I' in Me." But, there is an "M" and "E." Fuse those two letters together and, once again, you are left with ME. It all comes full circle. And, at the end of the day, isn't it really all about Me?

In hindsight, I may not have made much progress writing this book, but at least I know who I am. Hey, everyone! Look at me! I wrote a book!

from the author of I'm Right. Now Deal With It!
THERE'S NO 'I' IN
ME
(but I keep looking anyway)
A Narcissist's Journey to the
Center of Self-Centeredness
SCOTT BLOOM

THE END

Images used under licenses from 123Rf.com, Shutterstock.com, and iStock.com.

Pg7: "Le Moal Olivier/123rf.com"; Pg9: "iStock.com/mphillips007"&"Trinacria/Shutterstock.com"; Pg13: "Oliyy/Shutterstock.com"; Pg17: "Antonio Balaguer Soler123rf.com"; Pg19: "shooarts/Shutterstock.com"; Pg25: "Sergey Nivens/Shuttersock.com"; Pg27: "Miceking/123rf.com"; Pg30: "MonkeyBusinessImages/Shutterstock.com"; Pg33: "iStock.com/aurumarcus"; Pg37: Michael Gray/shutterstock.com; Pg41: "ZacariasPereiradaMata/Shutterstock.com"; Pg43: "Sabphoto/Shutterstock.com"; Pg47: "13_Phunkod/Shutterstock.com"; Pg49: "NASA images/Shutterstock.com"; Pg53: "spaxiax/Shutterstock.com" & "HongVo/Shutterstock.com"; Pg57: "Denis Ismagilov/123rf.com"; Pg59: "ChristianChan/Shutterstock.com"; Pg61: "Elnur/Shutterstock.com"; Pg65: "Richard Thomas/123rf.com"; Pg69: "MRAORAOR/Shutterstock.com."